Bader's Battle

Written and illustrated by
Mick Manning and Brita Granström

Collins

Douglas Bader was the most famous RAF fighter pilot of World War II. But he was a pilot with a difference …

Bader joined the RAF in 1928 and quickly became a skilful young flyer.

He was a high-flyer in other ways too: he was a good cricketer and footballer, and motorbike racer.

But he was also a bit of a show-off …

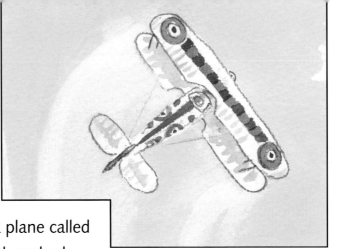

In 1931, while doing some stunts in a plane called a Bristol Bulldog … he lost control and crashed.

4

Bader was rushed to hospital.

The doctors discovered his legs were smashed to pieces. They had no choice; to save Bader's life they had to operate and cut off the remains of his legs.

I'm sorry, Douglas. It was the only way to save your life!

What kind of a life can I have with no legs? No sport … No driving … NO FLYING!

5

Bader spent weeks practising, putting up with terrible pain. Slowly he learnt to walk!

Bader even had his car changed so he could drive with his "tin legs".

Luckily his plane didn't need changing and Bader was excited to fly for the RAF again. Even though Bader had re-passed his flying test wearing his metal legs, the RAF didn't think a man with metal legs could be a skilful fighter pilot.

But Bader didn't give up.

Well, sir – can I be an RAF pilot?

I'm sorry, Bader, we don't think so.

Get your legs on, Douglas – we're flying today!

In 1939, World War II broke out. Worried that Nazi Germany might invade Britain, the RAF wanted as many fighter pilots as possible. Douglas was allowed to rejoin at last.

Douglas quickly learnt to fly the best RAF fighter planes: Hurricanes and Spitfires.

9

Every day enemy aircraft would fly over the sea to attack Britain. The RAF fighter pilots would race to their aircraft for take-off and go to meet the enemy.

It became known as the Battle of Britain.

By 1940, Bader had become a Squadron Leader and had shot down his first enemy aircraft.

By August 1941 he had shot down over 20 enemy aircraft. He was becoming famous – even in Germany.

12

One day, he was attacked over France by enemy fighters. His plane was hit. The tail broke off!

Bader tried to escape but one metal leg got stuck.

Suddenly, Bader's opening parachute broke the straps on his trapped leg and tugged him out of the diving Spitfire.

17

He was free … but not for long! He had left one metal leg behind in the plane, so when he landed in France he couldn't walk. He was soon captured by German soldiers.

The German fighter pilots had heard all about Douglas Bader and wanted to meet him.

18

Bader even persuaded the Germans to ask the RAF to send him a new leg. It was dropped by parachute in a wooden box!

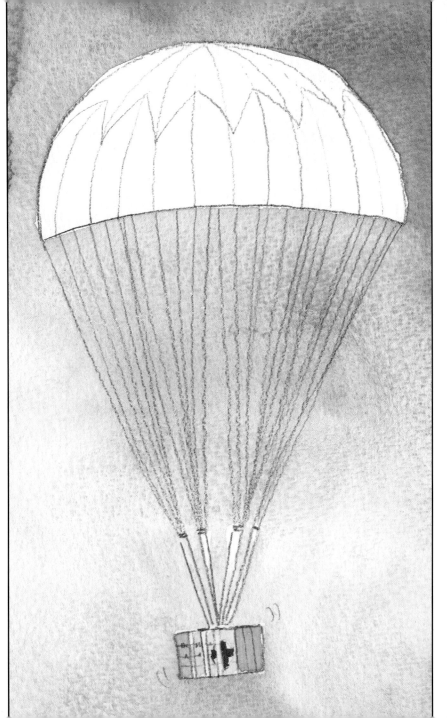

Once his leg arrived Bader put it on … and escaped out of a hospital window!

19

But he was soon captured once again by German soldiers.

Bader tried to escape many times. But on his metal legs he never got far. Eventually he was sent to a famous prisoner of war camp called Colditz.

Douglas Bader stayed at Colditz until he was freed by American troops near the end of the war.

After the war Douglas Bader left the RAF and worked to help disabled people – many injured by war. After he died in 1982 his family formed the Douglas Bader Foundation to help disabled people.

Bader's battles

Ideas for reading

Written by Gillian Howell
Primary Literacy Consultant

Learning objectives: *(reading objectives correspond with Gold band; all other objectives correspond with Diamond band)* read independently and with increasing fluency longer and less familiar texts; understand underlying themes, causes and points of view; understand how writers use different structures to create coherence and impact

Curriculum links: History, Citizenship

Interest words: accident, fighter pilot, control, operate, stubborn, balance, practising, skilful, Hurricanes, Spitfires, aircraft, Squadron, parachute, Colditz

Resources: pens, paper, internet

Word count: 705

Getting started

- Read the title together and discuss the cover illustration. Ask the children to say what they think the book will be about and when it is set.

- Turn to the back cover and read the blurb together. Check if the children's first thoughts were correct. Point out that Bader became the most famous fighter pilot in World War II and that this is a true story that has been fictionalised. Discuss what they already know about pilots in World War II.

- Turn to pp2–3 and point out that this is a graphic novel. Discuss what features the book will have, flicking through and pointing out the multiple frames and speech bubbles. Remind them that the illustrations and speech bubbles are important to the story and much of the story is told in the images.

Reading and responding

- Ask the children to read to the end of the book in pairs. Remind them to use their phonic knowledge and contextual clues to work out new words.

- Explain that as they read the book, you want them to make notes of key pieces of information or events that made him so famous.

- As they read, pause and ask the children to say what extra information they get from reading the speech bubbles. For example, on p18, ask what impression the speech bubbles give about the German officer's attitude to Bader.

Returning to the book

- Ask the children to turn to pp22–23 and recount the illustrated events in Bader's life from memory, discussing the battles he fought and how he overcame each one. Ask them to use their notes to highlight to the group which of these key moments made him famous.